Evanescent Reveries

A tapestry of chaotic dreams

Srijeet Sarkar

BookLeaf Publishing

India | USA | UK

Dedication

This book is dedicated to my father, the late Dr. Ranjit Sarkar, my mother Chandra Sarkar, my son Saatvik Dey Sarkar, my wife Sushmita Dey and my brother Dibyajeet Sarkar, for always being my *North Star*. Each of you has consistently inspired me to pursue my passions and to dream the impossible!

Acknowledgement

This book wouldn't have been possible without the unwavering support of those who have read and appreciated my work over time! Thank You for the motivation!

Preface

This book is a collection of my poems that touches on varied topics of life like - Purpose, Dreams & Love! I have tried to pour my soul out in words to describe my feelings towards all things endearing in life!

'INNOCENCE'

As we sit cosy,
And watch the world burn,
Is there anything at all we wish to—
Reminisce, rewind, or rerun?

Don't we yearn for those days,
When chasing fragrance knew no bounds,
And our free spirits cared only for—
Blooming flowers and joyful sounds!

Times when we raced after kites in the sky,
Dressed our Barbies, letting imaginations fly!

Those were the days when we understood the
real meaning of 'unity in diversity',
Shared lunches at school; made us realise the
essence of a true community!
Only "Mathematics" resonated with division's
true name,
As we savoured our moments together, free
from blame!

I wonder each day where that innocence has
flown,
What has been lost, while we have grown?
Tuning in to news, we witness the world's
growing pain,
Bloodshed in the name of caste, creed, and
gain!

Without a cringe, we outdo our own greed,
Lost in aggression, ignoring the need.
Each to their own—we fight for our right,
But in this chaos, we lose sight of the light!

Childhood innocence is now plagued by
resentment & judgement,
Growing into pessimists, devoid of
contentment!
Why don't we smile through our sorrows?
Questioning the ugly, and counting all our
borrows!

Like seeds sowed that fought hard to grow,
Where is all the humbleness we're meant to
show?
We love our country yet scorn its kin,
Adore our state but laugh at others' sin!

This hypocrisy isn't mature proverbial clarity,
Unless we grasp life in its true rarity.
No one is stopped from questioning their
faith,
But let's not lose sight of humanity's wraith.

Growing up should mean becoming more
humane,
Counting our blessings through boon or
bane!

Facing life's ostentation with an innocent grin,
Embracing the chaos without disdain!

For humanity now aches to reclaim that lost grace,
Those times when even life's most turbulent anecdotes found its rhythmic place!

'LUMINOUS RECKONING'

Burn your soul and spread the light,
Never back down; without putting up a fight!

The world may judge you, that's no surprise,
Live fully, and let go of the ties.

People will form their perceptions,
They may laugh at your imperfections.

But don't let their words define who you are;
Only you know the story behind your own
scar.

Choose to live, to love, and to laugh,
Remember, no dream is too small to craft.

Break free from the shackles of time and tide,
Rise above sorrows with wings spread wide.

For someday the blind will learn to see
What all of this was truly meant to be.

Until then..
Set your soul free; don't go gentle into the
night—
Burn bright, and continue to spread your
light!

'DOCILE DREAMS'

We wish to run,
We wish to fly,
Reaching for stars that glitter in the sky!

Blinded by wishes,
Broken dreams fail to scare;
The sharpest cuts on our souls no longer tear!

Yet still we seek the way ahead,
Ignoring the conscience that's smothered and
dead!

Is it that the memories no longer matter,
Or is organised chaos better than scattered
clatter?

Why can't we see that life beckons those who
care,
Not the ones who turn from their soul's
aching stare?

It's time for this generation to face adversity
head-on,
To embrace the storm after enjoying the
dawn!
Life isn't just about stressing to reach success,
It's also about living joyfully in the process!

Let's pledge to make memories that mark our
way,
For each day lived fully adds meaning to our
stay.

Meaningful relationships are the true wealth
we must seek,
Wanting the stars without shining makes the
soul weak!

So sort your sorrows by making others smile,
Let go of your ego; stay away from all the
guile!
Make no one your stepping stone to glory,
For each soul that enters your world has their
own story!

Live, love, and laugh to stay joyful and sane,
Don't lose your charm in a chase for material
gain.
As the clock ticks down, you'll come to know,
Real luxury always lies in having your loved
ones glow!

So hold them close, as they nonchalantly play
their part,
For in their warmth lies the joy of the heart!

'WHITE DOVE'

A new year and a new dream,
Life's story turns another blank page, echoing
humanity's scream!

In this usual rat race, it's just another day,
We look past love and the things we should
weigh.

How silly it is that we rush without pause,
Forgetting the joy of commitment and the
happiness it draws.

Pacing ahead, we chase wealth and gain,
Neglecting the respect that nurtures our own
fragile brains.

Small acts of joy no longer bring smiles,
Forgetting our trials, we're too busy counting
miles!

With humanity's eyes wide shut, the world
decays,
Our regressive mentality fuels chaos in
countless ways.

Pouncing like scavengers, we seek instant
thrill,
To us, consent and love are just irrelevant
frills.

Conscience blinded by greed, we've lost our
way,

What once was luxury is now deemed a
necessity each day!

Wasn't our upbringing meant to make us
humane?
Then what stops us from rising, from
breaking this chain?

In our comfort zones, we point fingers at
others,
Discussing the trivial; ignoring the stutters!

Poverty & injustice thrive in such a space,
From the poor to the powerful, all caught up
in the rat race.

People lose compassion in their quest for
materialistic love,
Peace no longer echoes the flight of the dove!

Each year brings change, but does it truly
align?
While dreams of the sane continue to resign.

Let's pledge for this year to be one of change,

Like a dark night waiting for the sun to
rearrange!

Rise as the 'Sons' you were meant to be,
Make your home and the world safe for her,
so dreams can run free!

Learn to be compassionate, spread love
without blame,
Play your part righteously; as we're all part of
the same game!

Let this year be filled with peace and
progressive love,
Resembling the elegance of a high-flying
dove.

'PAUSE & PLAY'

Let life take a beautiful pause,
As you go through your treasure trove—
A trove of unsung memories,
Of life and its incomplete stories!

Let them shape your will,
Helping you look forward with a convincing zeal.
A zeal to love as if you've never been hurt,

Embracing the essence that sees beyond the
dirt!

For life teaches lessons unknown,
With every dark day, a glimmer of hope is
sown.
So nurse your wounds and bring back that
smile,
Remember, it will be alright after a while!

Time and tide wait for none;
Every pitch-dark night gives way to the sun.
Make peace with your scars, wear them with
pride,
For they define the beauty of the battles
inside!

Wait benevolently for brighter days,
Your moment of glory will come in its own
ways!

Until then, display that radiant grin,
Face the world boldly; let hope always win.
Watch carefully as waves hit the shore,

In their retreat, you'll learn that life takes
away less & offers more!

Dance to life's rhythm, let it consume you,
For one day, all your dreams might just come
true!
Until then, spread the love that's truly due,
And patiently wait for karma to return it all
to you!!

'WHEN SHADOWS FADE'

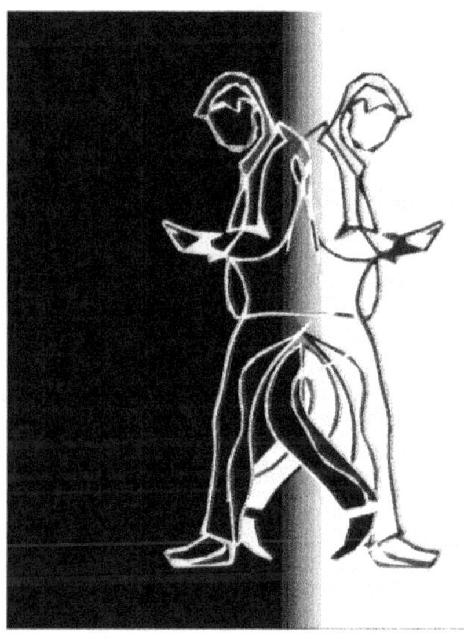

There are days when I'm not at my best,
Days when everything you believe in me is
put to the test!

There are days when I feel flawed and guilty,
Days when I am oblivious to the eminent
clarity.
Believe in me, even on those days,

No matter what the world does or says!

For love and hope are ours to weave,
The magic we fear lost is ours to retrieve!

There are days when I make you feel
spectacular,
Days when my grin seems a bit peculiar.
Days when I hug you tight and near,
And days when I make you feel completely
dear!

These are the moments I want you to hold on
to,
Remember them when darkness looms and
the night feels untrue!

For the tightest hugs come after the fiercest
fight,
And gloom always gives way to the brightest
light!

There are days when I may feel clumsy and
strange,
Days when I'm lost, in need of a change.

Remember to love me a little more then,
For it's in those moments I shall need you
again!

With a little love from both you and me,
Let's build that perfect world everyone
aspiringly wishes to see!

A world full of warmth, where we can be free,
In the beauty of our bond, just you and me!

'SYMPHONY OF STRIDES'

Who says you're not destined for greatness,
Just because they overlook your inner finesse?

Why bare your demons for the world to see,
And let others dictate your journey's decree?

Isn't it 'time to cast off the need for approval,

As you chase after dreams that are your own
fuel?
Your struggles are yours; let them not be
defined,
By those who don't see the fire in your mind!

Be your own hero; live fully, be bold,
Release the past's grip, let your story unfold!

For 'today' is the 'tomorrow' you worried
about 'yesterday',
So cherish each moment, let blessings pour
out everyday.
Ask a child who's lost, or a blind man with
dreams,
You'll see how your troubles are smaller than
they seem!

In life's vast tapestry, woven with care,
Each thread tells a tale of joy, pain, and flair.

So who says you're not destined for great
things?
Who are they to question the joy that hope
brings?

Each of us holds a gift, not for show or
display,
A sublime spark within, ready to light up the
way!

Take a moment to pause: live, laugh, and
share,
Ignore the naysayers; let your spirit
demonstrate the flare.

Happiness and struggle often dance hand in
hand,
This, my friend, is life's universal strand!

Learn to laugh each day, not at your own
plight,
But at those who doubt the brilliance of your
light!
They know nothing of the magnificent force,
That flows from within, bewilderingly
charting its own course!

So smile & continue striding forward; leaping
over your flaws,

Remember to breathe & take that critical
pause!
Contemplate life by keeping your essence
true,
One day you'll achieve the grand dreams
meant for you!

'MELANCHOLIC LIFE'

In a world transformed; we reluctantly find
our way,
Time spent at home, a bittersweet ballet!

Loved ones once taken for granted, are now
held dear,
Their warmth a beacon, their laughter sincere.

Yet shadows linger, as many continue to face
empirical loss,
Heart's heavy with sorrow, they bear the cost.

While some find solace in familiar embrace,
Others traverse grief in a hollowed space!

Irony reigns in our gadget-filled lives,
As certainty falters, and anxiety thrives.

The spectre of death dances close at hand,
Inviting us all to pause, in order to
understand!
For it spares none—rich or poor,
Evoking a mirage of emotions; reeking up a
feel,
As humanity's trials; become a starkly raw
reveal!

Perhaps it's a lesson, a call to reflect,
To cherish this moment, to truly connect!

As the present unfolds with its challenges
vast,

Let our vision of future embrace change,
holding steadfast.

Let us pledge to live & to amplify care,
Transforming our hearts, our lives, and our
share!

Let's reshape our existence, making love our
decree,
Reassess our desires, diligently seeking what
truly sets us free!

For if joy is anchored in what's yet to be,
We risk feeling lost, adrift in a sea!
Let's live full of laughter, making love our
guide,
Because procrastination of joy is indeed a
perilous tide!

May tales of the tooth fairy breathe hope into
our dreams,
As lovebirds remind us of life's tender
themes!
So let's embrace this journey, with hearts
open wide,

And cherish each moment, with audacious
love as our guide!

'SACRED SILENCE'

Holding hands, you guided our way,
Yet as we grew, the chase led us astray.

Money and success became our relentless
drive,
In the whirlwind of life, we often forget to
thrive.

Even now, as we stumble and fall,
A hand reaches out, with a familiar call:
"Watch out, my beloved! heed my gentle
plea,"
A voice filled with love, always there to see.

Amidst the chaos, we glance up and find
A comforting smile, a presence so kind!

She wears our torn shoes, selflessly so,
Hoping we'll prosper, as we learn and grow.

Yet we overlook this gesture, like countless
ones before,
Chasing forever; always wanting more!

And there she stands; with wrinkles that
show,
Longing for the child who has wandered
astray from home!

We're all busy chasing the dream job, the
dream car,
But would this pursuit hold meaning? like an
endless memoir!

If we fail to pause, to breathe, and reflect,
To cherish the one who has always been there
to protect?

She dressed us for school, packed lunches
with care,
Brushing our unruly hair with love beyond
compare.

Now life has given us time to sit and see,
To hold onto memories before they slip free!

So let's take a moment, let's hold them near,
Remember the lessons they taught us with
cheer.

Setting aside their own dreams to see us
flourish and thrive,
Cheering us on to become who we're meant
to be in our life.

It's time we pause, just a slight heartbeat
more,

To hug them back warmly, when they open
the door!

Let Mother's Day be a start, a gentle embrace,
A reminder to cherish, to honour & to grace.

'MEANDERING WINDS'

As the wind rushes past me, it whispers and calls,
Yet lost in my haste, I ignore all its thralls.
Racing through curves, I embrace the wild cheer,
With the thrill of the ride, I shed all my fear.

The distances I long for now seem to draw near,
Winding streets beckon brightly, their edges so clear.

The thunder of my bike sings a sweet, joyous
tune,
Nothing else in this world makes my spirit so
attune.

I speed past the mountains, snow-capped and
grand,
Saluting their majesty, I take a bold stand.
Above me, the clouds weave new paths in the
sky,
Charting journeys of wonder as I swiftly
zoom by.

In this moment, I awaken, with fresh eyes
aglow,
Questions swirl in the breeze, inviting
thoughts to flow.

Answers slowly arise, filling me with bright
fire,
Guiding me through life's unyielding
quagmire.

Life in itself is a fascinating race,

Where nature's embrace gives us strength and
a soothing place.

One wrong move could lead us to lose all
acclimatised grace,
Yet the docile heart in flight cannot be stalled
in pace!

For while the dream races pulse with delight,
The lessons we gather are treasures so bright!

Enchantingly tracing the paths that we roam,
Reminding us always to cherish what we left
behind as 'home'.

Let's not forget those who have been by our
side,
Who've lifted us up in our moments of pride.
As we forge ahead boldly riding the waves of
freedom alone,
Remember that the journey's much sweeter
when shared with someone known!

'INSATIABLE WISH'

If you wish for fame and find it near,
You also welcome jealousy and fear!
So I'll hold my wishes close to heart,
Not seeking glory, lest it tears me apart!!

If you long for wealth and see it flow,
You invite rudeness and arrogance to grow!
So I'll treasure simplicity instead,
Content with the joy that's easily spread!!

If you wish harm to others' plight,

You trade your peace for shadows in the
night!
So I'll choose compassion, being empathetic
and kind,
For in love's embrace, true strength I find!!

If ever I have a single wish to share,
It won't be for wealth or accolades to bear!
To be truly happy, my heart will strive,
For a world full of love where every single
human can thrive!!

'GRIT'

When there's a will,
There's surely a way—
Isn't that what they say?

As clouds gather round and thunder draws
near,
I pause in the moment, embracing my fear.
In this fleeting silence, I start to perceive,
Limitless wonders that I humbly believe.

Yet a thought stirs within me, a question
profound:
What if there's neither a will nor a way
found?
Where would we turn? Would we drift in
dismay,
Lost in this world's intricate play?

Then, with a resounding clap of thunder,
An answer shines bright, breaking through
the wonder.
Even when I stumble, I must rise once again,
With grit in my heart, I'll endure through the
pain!

For life is a journey yet to be conquered,
Each step a lesson, each moment a wonder.

So when I fall down, I'll bounce back up
higher,
Pressing on undeterred, fuelled by my fire!

Though the path may be narrow, with
obstacles near,
I refuse to give in; I shall face every fear.

With courage as my armour and hope as my
light,
I'll forge my own way, ready for the fight!

'FRIENDS INDEED'

Hold my hand, and I'll never let you go—
Some bonds last forever; that's all I wish for
you to know.

From strangers to friends, from unknowns to
kin,
Life took a sweet turn as our story began to
spin.

Every conversation shared, every feeling
stirred,
Helped me navigate the test of time,
unperturbed.

Fostering a bond, secure and sublime,
A treasure to cherish, a rhythm in rhyme.

So consider me a well-wisher for life,
A dear friend, steadfast, through both joy and
strife.
And I promise you—no tears of regret,
As this friendship shall construe to be an
invaluable asset!

As the years roll by, we'll grow old with grace,
I promise to still laugh at your silly jokes,
accepting the flaws with an embrace.

For years from now, no matter where we
roam,
Whether happy or lost, you'll always feel like
home!
You'll be someone I shall always strive to see,
A cherished friend, an extended part of me!

I've heard that some friendships are never
diminished,
And that's how I want ours—to be loved and
cherished!

'REMEMBER'

Try falling asleep
Before you fall apart.
For every pain that stirs anew
Needs a kind, consoling heart.

Life dances between
Sinful joy and regret,
So cradle your dreams gently,
With your eyes firmly set.

Don't let your visions shatter,
Though they may seem threadbare;
If you choose to forsake what you hold,
Tread diligently with care!

Life moves ever onward,
Yet leaves its haunting trace,
Memories left unclaimed
Drift in forgotten space.

Oh, how we long
For life to be a simple song,
Like in the films, where feelings blend;
harmonious and strong!

So stop before you surrender,
Don't let go without putting up a fight;
Every soul deserves
A second chance lurking in their sight.

Hold onto those who matter,
Craft memories that gleam;
In the end, don't fumble through the pieces
Of your own shattered dream!

Live each day fully,
Express all that you ever could!

For if it still hurts;
Try falling asleep,
Before you fall apart—
For every pain that resurrects
Needs a consoling heart!

'BRAND NEW STORY'

Come, let's write a brand new story,
A world without pain, dread or worry!

A place where right and wrong gently fade,
Where all of us join in a beautiful serenade.

Hand in hand, we walk the path of love,
Free from judgement from anyone above.

Imagine a realm where each world is bright,
Where even the thought of pain doesn't feel
right!

Where freedom soars like a bird seldom
caged,
And every emotion flows, unengaged.

A life rich in empathy, not in greed,
Where kindness blossoms, and hearts take the
lead!

A world so perfect that 'hunger' ceases to have
a name,
Where all 'religions' resonate with peace, and
not acts of shame!

So come, let's unite and pen this new tale,
Loving each other & letting the lost glory
prevail!
Gleefully helping one another heal,
Earning goodwill on karma's vibrant wheel!

'LEAP OF FAITH'

Take a leap of faith in this world of grey,
For clarity's a fleeting dream that constantly
slips away.

Know that 'right' and 'wrong' are nothing but
judgements we make,
Clouded by notions that our true selves
forsake.

While we yearn for a life free from hate,
The violence we harbour seals our own fate!

Rushing through the rat race, we strive to
keep pace,
As humanity suffers in the chaos we chase.

Anticipating harmony with every stride,
Yet 'faith' becomes a divider, not a source of
pride!

Before our era fades into distant lore,
Let's promise to stumble, but never ignore.

Let's give each other reasons to hold our
heads high,
To walk tall in the face of a questioning sky.

Let's earn goodwill by spreading love and
respect,
Making amends for the years of neglect.

No longer shall we sit and watch the world
burn,

It's time to rise up and protect what we
yearn!

Standing firm against injustice, for ourselves
and our kin,
Leading by example, let true change begin!

Though efforts may falter and dreams may
feel frail,
Hold on tight, for this journey is fraught with
a trail.

So take that leap of faith in this world of grey,
For clarity may elude us, but hope continues
to light up the way.

'POURING RAIN'

The pouring rain stirs deep within our souls,
The gusting wind whispers ancient tales as it
rolls.

A symphony of nature, the raindrops play,
While petrichor calls us back to yesterday!

Yet as gentle rains shift to a fierce storm,
What once felt essential can lose its warm.

As waters rise and calm gives way to strife,
We long for the end of this turbulent life.

Just like our journeys, we start with zest and
zeal,
But when tides turn against us, we question
what's real.

Why do we fear the thunder's mighty roar?
Why not trust that sunshine will follow once
more?

Patience is the virtue we must hold dear,
For the soul must learn to trust, cleanse, and
persevere.

Time and tide wait for none; this we know,
Each moment of patience gives us a chance to
grow.

So wait & let hope be a beacon; bright and
rare,
As we cultivate a world filled with genuine
care.

Through every storm, may we rise and inspire,
Creating a life that lifts us ever higher!

In the dance of the elements, we learn to
adapt,
Navigating chaos, our spirits unwrapped.

With hearts intertwined, we shall brave the
downpour,
Humanity standing tall together, ready to
face any shore!

'PARENTAL BLISS'

As dusk descends and night draws near,
A soft, faint cry takes flight, so dear.
Tiny hands reach out, eager to play,
Gently urging us to guide their way.

In whispers shared, we tell our tales,
Of joy and wonder, of winds and sails.

Teaching our little one to be brave, to be
strong,
Nurturing the spark that grows into a song.

In those innocent eyes, so bright, so true,
A beaming smile greets the world anew.
Through sleepless nights and busy days,
This joyful chaos steals our gaze.

We cheer as they wander, explore the
unknown,
Fostering courage, love brightly sown.
With scraped knees and laughter sweet,
In each small triumph, our hearts repeat.

Amid the chaos, doubts, and lessons spun,
Their passion burns like the setting sun.
For one day, their tiny hand will outgrow
ours,
But we'll cherish the seed that bloomed into
flowers!

'BON VOYAGE'

The twists of the road stretch far and wide,
Paving paths where dreams and hearts reside.
With every turn, a world anew,
Waiting in silence—just for you.

Trees dance in the breeze with grace,
While mountains bear history on their face.
The river's song—a gentle tune,
As the night sky glows beneath the moon.

Through cities we wander, the air alive,
Each corner whispers tales that thrive.
In crowded streets and quiet lanes,
Lives unfold, with a thousand names.

Beneath the stars, we lie and dream,
Seeking places not found on any map or
scheme.
Not on pages, but in moments bright,
Beyond the cages of the day and night.

From sunlit shores to deserts wide,
Through mountains tall and oceans' tide,
Each journey sparks the heart's desire—
A flame that burns, an endless fire.

Along the way, the moments are full,
We carry love home, hearts brimming and
full.
A piece of earth, a slice of sky,
And memories that will never die.

'ENDEARING PROCLIVITY'

The world keeps turning, blind to the cry,
As humanity sighs, waiting to ask, *why?*
Are we waiting for a grand reveal?
With hearts grown cold, no words can heal.

But in a simple gesture, kind and true,
We can make the world feel fresh and new.
Like the sun's first light breaking the night,
Turning shadows to gold, and dark to bright.

Let kindness echo as love's clear sound,
Let your presence bring peace all around.
No need for grand gestures, no need for a
show,
It's in how we listen, how we truly know.

Seek out the ones who need your embrace,
Make this world kind, a truly beautiful place.
Honour every promise you've made in this
life,
And let no one be alone in moments of strife.

What the world needs is simple and true,
An endearing proclivity, soft as the dew.
A peaceful force, gentle as a breeze;
That whispers its love with effortless ease!
It's in how we bring peace, no need to strive,
A quiet reminder of what it means to be alive.

'VOX POP'

Life has turned into a constant stream,
Racing by, like a half-baked dream.
Everything reduced to a screen's bright light,
Where moments are captured, but out of
sight.

We snap our selfies, we post our lives,
Surrounded by strangers, yet nobody arrives.
Lost in the crowd, still unseen,
Hearts are measured by the size of a screen.

"Like," "share," "subscribe"—a hollow praise,
The digital world never leaves our gaze.
Seeking approval from voices that don't care,
Sharing our souls, but still unaware.

We wear opinions like a virtual shroud,
Loud in the silence, lost in the crowd.
We find our voices, but who's around
To truly hear, to truly be found?

We scroll through posts, chasing the light,
But forget what we need most: to reconnect,
To lift our gaze beyond the glass,
To listen, not just hear, to embrace the
contrast.

For in the end, it's not the likes we chase,
But the real connections that light up our
grace.
The human touch, the face-to-face,
This is what fills our hearts and leaves a
lasting trace.

'EPHEMERAL REFLECTIONS'

Beneath the tremor of a whispered breath,
Echoes rise from the edge of death.
Not as nightmares, but as bubbles bright,
Trapped in the shadows of fading light.

Striking a chord like fleeting dreams,
Soft as shimmers on moonlit streams.
Each wish turns into a prayer,
Rising from raised hands into the air!

Effervescent in their own way,
Captivating the thoughts that drift away.
Bedazzled by the sparkle of distant stars,
Fading softly like forgotten scars.

Each reverie, vanishing without trace,
Like a thousand distorted faces in time and
space.
In a world where unsung words
melodramatically sing,
Caught in the echoes of an unfurled wing.

Like the taste of fine wine lingering on the
tongue of night,
It burst into flavours of soft delight,
Leaving behind the view of vivid skies,
Beneath the breath of hopeful dreams that
never die.

'FLICKERS OF A FLEDGLING SOUL'

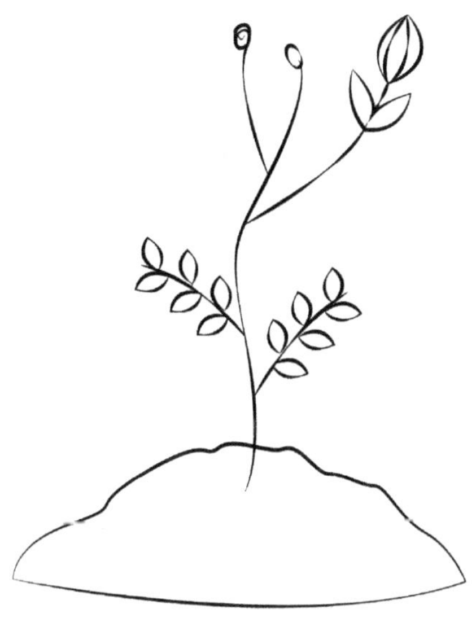

At the shores of the ocean where wild winds
play,
We built our castles from sand and clay!
With multicoloured skies and paper wings,
We soared above the clouds of doubt, doing
unimaginable things.

The world was a playground; ours to take,

Each dusk turning to dawn, each drop
saturating the lake.
Paddling through the streams of hope,
Heart watching the universe dance through
its periscope.

The moon was ours to climb and touch,
The stars were ours to hold and clutch.
We spoke to the sun, sang to the light,
And danced with shadows until the night.

Each day we discovered a new key,
To lands where we could truly be—
Lands with brave knights and secret spies,
Surrounded by fireflies that lit our eyes.

The clock would move; but time stood still,
We caught each day; chasing dreams to fulfil.
The wish was always to not wake up too soon,
To live forever beneath the glowing moon!

Now those dreams are faint whispers,
Like echoes on a canvas that surrenders.
Yet sometimes, in the quiet of the night,
I hear them speak to me as I sleep tight.

'REALM OF REALITIES'

Once, we chased flying kites,
Looking amusingly at the skies;
The world seemed awake; the roads seemed
free,
Every song had an enchanting melody.

But time, like a free-flowing river; pulls us
near,
Whispering softly into our ear; that we must
move on and continue to steer!
Winds that once were wild and bold,
Now carry the weight of responsibilities;
worth the price of gold!

We learn to hold dear both love and pain,
To dance in the sun and soak in the rain!
With sturdy hands and dreams refined,
We try to pick up the crumbles of the shatter
we left behind.

As the carefree laugh begins to fade,
Replaced by choices we need to make!
The bills and duties usher in the dread,
Crossing paths, we need to sombrely tread.

Yet in the quiet of the night,
There stirs a hopeful spark of light.
Even as the burdens grow,
The hopeful heart still looks forward to glow.

For growing up isn't an easy one,
A journey where we constantly unlearn and
learn.
Highest of highs and lowest of falls,
Rising again effortlessly through it all!

So let the grey hair be shown,
Let it guide you in a crowd; never leaving you

alone.
For with each step, no matter how small it
seems,
We carry nonchalantly the weight of our
dreams.

'ECHOES OF BEING'

Beneath the stars on a pitch-dark night,
Where thoughts ebb and flow from left to right.
The undercurrents soft; yet deep and wide,
As contemplation rises with every tide.

What is life, if not a fleeting breath?
Isn't it a dance of joy, with a touch of death?
Are we the echoes of our past,
Or fleeting shadows of the future that won't last?

I wonder if the stars know,
What to hold on to and what to let go?
We carry hopes, both frail and bright,
Like candles flickering on a stormy night.

With every step, a story's told,
In every tear, a truth unfolds.
And yet we search with yearning eyes,
For meaning in these vast, dark skies.

Who defines the path we take?
Or does the wind of fate help us stay awake?
Are we the artists, or mere clay?
Following the course or led astray?

Perhaps the answer floats in air,
Amid moments lived by hearts that care.
For knowing that the roads we roam
Can either lose us or guide us home.

So, gazing up, we stitch our story,
In the quiet hum of life's great mystery.
For this future isn't a puzzle resolved,
Unless we have what it takes to be evolved.

'THE TRIUMPH IN THE TUMBLE'

The road to glory twists and bends,
A path that curves with no true ends.
We stumble first, then rise once more,
In every bruise, there's a lesson to explore.

Failure precariously burns deep,
But from this very soil, there's wisdom we
reap.
Each misstep marks a ground to tread,

A blueprint for breaching the fortress ahead.

Take the tallest tree or strongest beams,
Both are forged in storms and built on
dreams.
The chaotic heart that beats and the hands
that bleed,
Know the true symphony of unmet need!

Success is not a fleeting flight,
But standing firm for what is right.
It's not found in the agony or disdain,
But in the lessons learned from immense pain.

For what is growth, if not the climb?
A testimony, timeless and sublime.
The cracks we wear, the scars we share,
Are the stories that make our success rare!

So, stumble with open eyes,
Since in each fall, a new hope lies.
Someday eventually you'll see it clear;
That Success was built by facing all that you
fear!

'SERENITY IN MOTION'

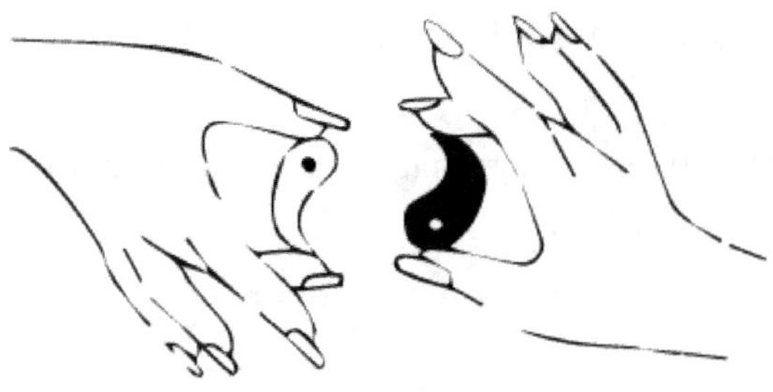

In the dance of dusk and dawn,
Shadows stretch as the light is nearly gone.
Somewhere here lies the truth in the soft
divide,
Splitting the two halves of the turbulent tide.

Yin, the quiet one, exudes grace,
Worshipping the moon with a silver face.
A subtle descent, both slow and deep,
Awakening feelings long asleep.

Yang, the sun, burns with vibrant might,
Bursting forth in dawn's first light.
A pulse that stirs the sleeping earth,
A melody calling the soul to birth.

One cannot stand without the other,
Like storms that follow calm, each unlike the
other.
It's in the dark that light finds its spark,
In silence, sound leaves its mark.

In balance, they exist, eternally entwined,
The soft and fierce, seeking peace in the wild.
For eventually, both light and dark will find
their way,
Night surrenders gently, ushering in the day.

In the balance of soft and strong,
We find our place, where we belong.
Though tempting are the paths of right and
wrong,
Never let good or bad decisions linger for too
long.

'DANCING WITH THE SECONDS'

The strands of time keep flowing unaware,
Following our imprints everywhere!
It runs through endless days,
Even as serendipity wears down in the
sharpest of ways.

A clock that notes the things unseen,
Shifts the shadows rapidly cast in between.
In this space, where moments breathe and
die,

Dreams surrender, then learn to fly!

Reverberating the ache in every heart,
The distant rhythm slowly tears us apart.
Marching on, it never stands still,
Conquering mountains, climbing every hill.

Yet we chase it, like the wind's embrace,
While it glides away with timeless grace.
Perched like a bird that nests out of our
reach,
Teaching volumes in silence without a speech!
For time is not a thing we own,
It arises from what is reaped and sown.
Like a stream that flows into the sea,
A dance of destiny, showcased for you and
me.

Slipping through fingers, lightning fast,
The moments linger, deep and vast.
Time, in truth, is never really gone,
It continues to reside beyond the boundaries
of right or wrong!

'VEILS OF VANITY'

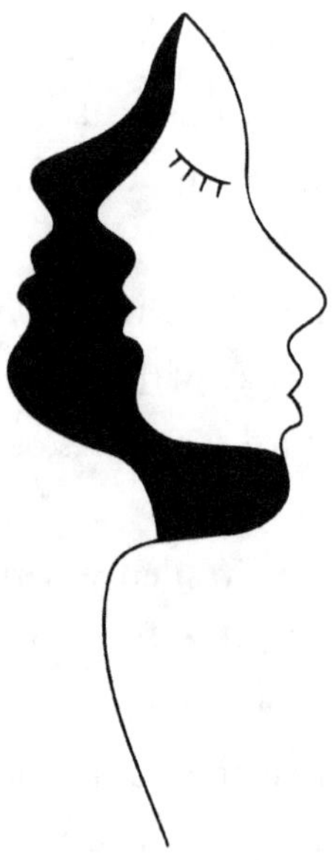

The glitter of gold showcases flashy pride,
Empty hearts have a pocketful to hide!
Ostentation wears a crown too bright,
A masquerade that keeps away the light.

Like a cloak of wealth radiating flawless
gleam,
Suppresses the silent cry beneath the dream!
Frivolous words pour in loud and grand,

Echoes of which are heard across the mosaic
land!

Eyes dazzle with every glance,
Showing a fleeting but hollow dance.
Where worth is measured by an exuberant
show,
While shallow roots no longer grow.

The jewels sparkle, but do not shine,
For what's displayed is not divine!
The universe doesn't conspire with the gilded
kings,
Who display their crowns on fragile strings.

Priceless things in life can never be bought,
They're found in what's not sold or sought.
Ostentation does have our momentary
attention,
But will soon fade with time, without a
meritorious relation!

As true worth lies in silent grace,
Let's not get blinded by the sparkle of an
empty space.

So wear your genuine heart on the sleeve;
Let actions speak the story you weave!
For in this quest of unfurling the veils of
vanity,
Let's embrace our own authenticity.

'ECLIPSES OF LIFE'

Life is an endless ocean, wide and deep,
Where seasons shift as silent changes creep.
From spring's first breath to winter's call,
We dance through destiny that enthrals us all.

The youthful days are bright and new,
Like blossoms kissed by morning dew.
The air is sweet with hope's embrace,
And dreams are spun in an endless space.

Then summer brings its blazing sun,
Marking the time that has just begun.

We race to outgrow our destinies fast,
Chasing shadows, trying to make memories
last.

Autumn unfolds both high and low,
As amber leaves begin to glow.
They light up our lives with their gracious
sway,
Teaching us critical lessons along the way.

Slowly, the branches turn bare, and the winds
grow cold,
Yet in the stillness, there are stories to be
told!
Of lessons learned and paths now clear,
Of wisdom found through the changing year.

Through spring, summer, fall, and frost,
We acknowledge what's gained, learned, and
lost.
In the end, it's for all to observe and see,
How each experience nourishes life's
effervescent tree.

'DEWDROPS OF DELIGHT'

There's magic in the minuscule things,
Like a bird that soars on quiet wings.
Morning mist gives way to the sunlit ray,
As leaves dance in their playful ballet.

The taste of coffee, warm and deep,
Laughter shared, knocking on hearts that
don't sleep.
The petrichor of soil, or rustling pages of a
book,
Or even a radiant smile accompanied by

stillness in a calm look.

Little things like having a hand to hold,
Or the sky turning pink and bold.
The soft embrace of evening's glow,
Where, amidst the whispers, time moves slow!

Life unfurls into joyful moments like a drizzle
on bare skin,
A feeling of wholeness returning within.
What speaks to us in volume is the silence of
the night,
The simple joy of being asked, "Are you
feeling alright?"

For life is not about grand displays,
But the little things shown in tender ways.
The simplest joys come from the softest
touch,
The memories that only give, without asking
for too much.

Slow your pace, and let these moments
breathe,
Enjoy the ride, and earnestly believe!

Simple joys of life aren't far away,
They're just waiting for a reveal at the dawn
of each new day!